Drawn to the Light

Drawn to the Light

Poems on Rembrandt's Religious Paintings

MARILYN CHANDLER McENTYRE

Marilyn Chandler McEntyre

WILLIAM B. EERDMANS PUBLISHING COMPANY
GRAND RAPIDS, MICHIGAN / CAMBRIDGE, U.K.

D RAWN TO THE L IGHT
Poems on Rembrandt's Religious Paintings
Text copyright © 2003 by Marilyn Chandler McEntyre
All rights reserved
Published 2003 by Wm. B. Eerdmans Publishing Company
255 Jefferson Ave. S.E., Grand Rapids, Michigan 49503 /
P.O. Box 163, Cambridge CB3 9PU U.K.
Printed in the U.S.A.
08 07 06 05 04 03   7 6 5 4 3 2 I

Library of Congress Cataloging-in-Publication Data
McEntyre, Marilyn Chandler, 1949–
    Drawn to the light: poems on Rembrandt's religious paintings / Marilyn Chandler McEntyre.
        p. cm.
    ISBN 0-8028-1282-I (hardcover: alk. paper)
    I. Rembrandt Harmenszoon van Rijn, 1606–1669—Poetry. 2. Bible—History of Biblical
events—Poetry. 3. Christian art and symbolism—Poetry. 4. Religious poetry, American. 5. Painting—
Poetry. I. Title.

PS3563.C3616D73 2003
813'.6—dc22

                                        2003060741

Book designed by Willem Mineur

www.eerdmans.com

Dedication

For my mother, Mary,
who first taught me to love the Bible

and for John,
whose delight in Rembrandt is a gift to me

Acknowledgments

I have been very grateful in the course of writing these
poems for the generous readings they have received, and the
encouragement I've been given by many along the way.
In particular I want to thank Paul Willis and Jo Carson
for the time and care they've given my poems;
Mary Hietbrink for her patient editing;
and, as always,
John, whose skills in seeing, listening, reading,
and revision are a constant
and precious gift.

COVER

Self-Portrait as the Apostle Paul, c. 1661, Rijksmuseum, Amsterdam, Holland

FRONTISPIECE

Detail of *The Return of the Prodigal Son,* c. 1668, Scala/Art Resource, NY

DEDICATION PAGE

Detail of *Hannah and Samuel,* c. 1648, Duke of Sutherland Collection,
on loan to the National Gallery of Scotland

Drawn to the Light

Table of Contents

Introduction

WHEN MY HUSBAND AND I spent a week in Amsterdam some years ago, we found ourselves, like most tourists at cheese-laden breakfast tables in Dutch "guesthouses," thumbing through guidebooks and considering options: walks by canals; bike rides among the windmills; visits to fishing villages, Anne Frank's house, the Resistance Museum. We did some of those things, but inclination and deepening fascination led us almost daily back to two of the great pilgrimage spots of Dutch art: the Rijksmuseum and Rembrandt's house. We were, in a very literal sense, drawn to the light.

The particular golden light that emerges out of ambient darkness in Rembrandt's paintings (and those of his pupils, to give a proper nod to the controversies still simmering over authentication) evokes something more than admiration for his technical skill. Unlike the daylight, twilight, or fluorescent lamplight we inhabit, unlike even the candlelit interiors of the thick-walled seventeenth-century canal houses where the artist and his contemporaries leaned over meals and maps and leather-bound books, this light burns with the energy of living presence. Human figures and the objects of daily life seem not only illumined but blessed by the light that envelops them, as though it comes from a source beyond the sun, and what it touches is made sacred.

The fact that so many of Rembrandt's subjects are biblical certainly attests to his recognition of the power of biblical stories to speak to us, but it is his light shining in darkness that convinces me even more powerfully of a mind and sensibility that dwelt long and longingly on the mystery of divine presence — and absence. Figures like the two apostles in his "Peter and Paul Disputing," for instance, deeply occupied with their own urgent questions, seem oddly unaware of the radiance that surrounds them,

turning their books to gold and burnishing their skin. Yet the room where they sit is transformed by an energy not entirely accounted for by a high window and the afternoon sun. The light that singles them out in a darkened chamber where winter cold closes in just beyond its touch works like dramatic irony: we see something they don't. Being outside the radiance they inhabit, we may recognize it as a shaft of grace that points as sharply as Peter's extended finger to the sacred Word as the center of attention.

I thought of this painting and of the luminosity that suffuses so many of Rembrandt's images recently when a pastor pointed out how often God is identified with light in Scripture. Though the identification may be metaphorical, I tend to think it pushes the boundaries of metaphor toward a literal recognition of the embracing, encompassing character of light itself — the absolute that manifests itself as the "rosy-fingered dawn" of the ancient Greeks, or the starlight that led shepherds to Bethlehem, or the "sudden shafts of sunlight" in Eliot's late poetry that leave one feeling visited.

Even the paintings with secular or pagan subjects in Rembrandt's oeuvre seem to draw from and specifically comment upon biblical descriptions of the human condition. "The people who sat in darkness have seen a great light, and for those who sat in the region and shadow of death, light has dawned" (Matthew 3:16). "The light shines in the darkness, and the darkness has not overcome it" (John 1:5). "He has called us out of darkness into his marvelous light" (1 Peter 2:9). These Dutch burghers huddling in chilly inner rooms, peering from the shadows, do sit in darkness, but they are singled out, held, and beatified by a light that intrudes its incongruous glory into their winter evenings.

The world of these paintings is as paradoxical as the mysterious assurance "The kingdom of God is among you" — or as the "already but not yet" language with which theologians teach us to think about our living in this "time between the times," citizens both of this world and of the kingdom. The light that shines in Rembrandt's dark world is a hint and a prom-

ise of something heavenly that is already actual here in the midst of murky and inglorious surroundings.

Like the people he painted, Rembrandt lived in the shadows. He lived through the darkness of Dutch winters and in the shadows of sickness and death, losses both personal and public. Few diseases were curable in the seventeenth century. Infants died routinely; women died in childbirth; plague lurked in living memory. Though this was what historians call Holland's "Golden Age," for many life was as Hobbes described it: "nasty, brutish, and short." Many of Rembrandt's contemporaries in the art world nevertheless gloried in the things of this world, perhaps took comfort in them — the rich trove of material goods made available by the wide reach of Dutch mercantile ships and new navigational technology. Most of us have paused somewhere to admire the technical precision of a perfectly rendered lemon peel hanging from a laden table, or a figured carpet whose folds look strikingly three-dimensional, or a silver pitcher gleaming with metallic sheen that transforms the canvas behind it. But in Rembrandt's paintings the things of this world are subordinated to something more worth seeing. The material environment is alluded to in the layers of period clothing, the jewels in a bride's hair, the lace on a young man's collar. But it is the liveliness of human presence — and something beyond that — which subordinates all objects to its ambiance. The best of the paintings show us life, manifest and mysterious, shadowed and radiant.

Much of that sense of life made manifest emerges, of course, in the portraits. Especially in the faces of old people — for instance, those of his mother in various guises and, later, his aging self — we see a quality of attention, reflection, awareness, and even amusement that reminds me of Adrienne Rich's wonderful phrase, "hard-won lucidity." They glow with the power of distilled experience. They comfort me in my own midlife: age is not something simply to be dreaded but a season that, if it is granted to us, may be a time of recollection in the deepest sense, of gathering and going inward, dwelling in quiet light, having learned to accept and integrate the shadow.

To visit Rembrandt's house even now, with its rows of etchings hung in indirect lighting in temperature-controlled rooms, is to imagine one's way back to an enclosed world where daylight was a precious commodity and where objects in corners and hallways were shrouded in permanent shadow. The etchings, a few paintings, and the tools of his craft on display are only part of what one may see and learn from there. The rooms themselves, the narrow hallways, the way one emerges suddenly from shadow into light, rounding a corner or emerging from a stairwell into a place where a window stretches upward to receive what sun is available, give at least a hint of how light may be cherished as a precious substance, and sought, and saved, like gold, in the mind and on the painter's brush.

It is the artist's vocation to surprise us into remembering that the ordinary elements of our messy, material lives are gifts. Rembrandt restores us to a sense of the sacramentality of daily life. This daily life provides the terms in which he "reads" the biblical stories and invites us to read them — moments of real encounter among real people working out their salvation with a God who made and makes himself known in palpable, visible, surprising ways. Their faces tell stories of sorrow and struggle and hard-won understanding; an insistent light has broken into the dark rooms and landscapes they inhabit. Emerging out of so much ambient shadow, these figures remind us to give thanks for the light we live by, even in the darkest times.

MARILYN CHANDLER MCENTYRE

Self-Portrait

(1628)

He painted his own image year after year,
tracing time with a fine-haired brush
as smooth planes dried to folds
and light shifted and shadows deepened.
He learned how the dark defines
what can be seen.

He fueled his fascination with the human face
by gazing on his own, learning, feature
by feature, how to touch each curl
with heartbreaking tenderness, how to treat
the lace at the throat with a delicacy
that honored the hand that wove it,
how to make the fine mustache, merest
hint of manhood, a token of dignity.

The young man emerging in half-light
like a child waking from dreams too old
for telling seems already to bear the weight
of sorrows foreseen, or cares that will call him
from his work and wake him in the night.
Yet delight remains in the self-imposed limits
of reds and browns and sparing gold,
the strokes, already masterly, of a brush
over which he must have bent
like an herbalist over a seedling, a lover
over his woman, or a midwife
over a newborn child.

Not every model can look so unobserved.

This placid unconcern over bare thighs
and loose breasts, intimate indifference
to the painter's presence, suggests
a woman so sure of being loved, she can forget
the lover's gaze and let him see her
all alone.

A Woman Bathing

Paradox of solitude seen,
movement caught and stilled,
light emerging from the ambient dark,
she is as real as memory or dream.

This is not pose, but pleasure.
She is Eve before something in Adam's eye
sent her into hiding. Miriam wading
near her brother's basket,
careless and safe. Ruth after gleaning,
cooling her grateful feet at the water's edge
before nightfall drew her, bathed and ready,
to Boaz's tent.

He really meant to do it.
All it took was an angel's merest touch
to stop him, but the boy's hands
were tied, the father's fingers
wrapped around his jaw
(perhaps to smother him — one paltry act
of mercy before the fatal slice?).

Abraham and Isaac

What kind of God would require
such appalling fidelity?
What kind of father could bear
to imagine the blade
leaving its trail of red
on the tender skin of a throat
no beard has covered?

What would it take?

What must be the magnitude
of a love that would go this far?
The look in Abraham's eye
is crazed. The angel's message
relieves him (though all his life
some madness will haunt him,
and Sarah will follow his steps
with darkened eyes):

You don't have to do this
any more. Another father
will take your place.

Another son will be led to slaughter.
The promise will be fulfilled,
Israel's seed will be planted.

Let him grow old and die.

Jacob's Struggle with the Angel

All night they wrestle, locked
in an embrace.

Sheltered by outspread wings,
Jacob leans into the struggle
like a child dreaming
on a mother's lap, thrashing
out his nightmare
while one loath to awaken him
holds him safe.

Wounded, he still hangs on.
Where else would he go?
Here, in the grip of fear
where nothing he knows by day
can save him, he finds his strength.

Self-abandoned, sweating, and asleep,
he is becoming Israel.
In the grip of desire he dares
to demand what only love can give.

Blessing comes at daybreak.
He limps into Canaan on a trembling thigh.

Jacob Blessing Joseph's Sons

Do not be deceived by the tremors of old men
or by their blindness.

Jacob sees more than his son
imagines, who urges his erring hand
toward Manasseh.

Jacob, we read, resisted.
Joseph, we read, was displeased:

"Not so, my father: for this is the firstborn;
put thy right hand upon his head."

But Jacob laid his hand on Ephraim's head
"wittingly." The old man still wears an animal's skin:
still the "hairy man," who has wrestled
with angels and a houseful of contending sons.

The painter, gentle reader, finds more tenderness
than turmoil in the young man's touch,
the old man's reach, the mother's acquiescent gaze.

The grandfather's fingers, almost hidden, caress
the cheated child nestled by his heart.

How strangely the Almighty honors
our petty plans, mistakes, manipulations,
hammering them into
swords and ploughshares.

The old story of stealth is reconciled in repetition.
"I know," Jacob says. "I know."

Even the troubled child, born first, blessed second,
will live to know how, despite our designs,
filial feuds, misplaced proprieties,

the fathers will be honored, the mothers vindicated,
and the seed of the sons scattered into nations
upon whom blessing sometimes lies heavy as a curse.

Moses Breaking the Tablets of the Law

Scholars still mourn
the burning of a thousand scrolls
at Alexandria.

Architects remember, bereft,
Dresden before the war,
Hiroshima's delicate pagodas.

Who among us
has not flinched at this:
sacred stone tablets,
handwritten by God,
lying in rubble at Moses' feet?

A second thought
in that moment of fury
(for posterity, for what
we would — surely — have treasured)
might have saved them.

He lifts them high and stands
one fatal moment, torn with rage,
disappointed once again
by the ragged mob
he's brought this far. (For what?

They don't even look up
from their whores' thighs, their jugs
of wine, the comforting campfires.
They saw no light on the mountain.)

He can't speak — words rattle
in a dry brain still buzzing
with the shock of a voice like thunder,
lightning carving letters in stone.

Speechless, he looks down on his people:
What you do not deserve, he decides,
I will destroy. Not one of you fools
will ever see God's perfect Aleph,
jots and tittles fine as the veins
on a fig leaf.

If you will not see, perhaps
you can hear the sound of rock, crushed
and tumbling down the mountainside.

The patron refused the canvas.
The painter cut it up.
Only the figure of Moses remains, furious,
choked with futility, ready to cast down
these stones before swine.

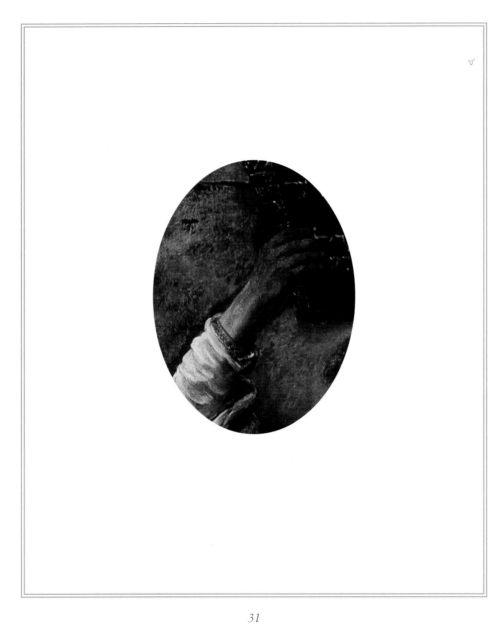

Hannah
and
Samuel

She longed for him.
She let him go.
Once a year, in the temple,
he kneels by her side,
a gift, a torment.

Long since weaned
to worship, he prays,
confident, unconscious
as a fledgling about to fly.

She turns her gaze inward,
remembering her weeping,
her promise, the slaughtered bull,
the flour, the wine, leaving him
in Eli's arms. Every year
she retraces every step
and leaves him behind once more.

One day another woman,
relinquishing her son,
will remember Hannah's lonely
choice, considering the difference
between curse and blessing.

The Reconciliation of David and Absalom

David's embrace is tentative.
Yet what can he do but embrace
this abject son of Cain,
flesh of his flesh?
He has no stones to throw.

Absalom weeps
on his father's breast.

If the story stopped there,
the sermon would be easy:
Repent and be forgiven.
Kill the fatted calf.
Welcome the prodigal home.

But the story goes on.
The tears dry, the heart hardens,
and the father, twice betrayed,
unreconciled at last, is left
to weep in his turn:
"Absalom, my son!
Would God I had died for thee!"

A prayer with an answer
as large as life.

What father would not die to bring back
even the worst of his children?

Simeon
with the
Christ Child
in
the Temple

How light he lies
in these ancient arms.
The infant's eyes open
to meet the old man's
as they close.

I have seen his eyesight fade.
I have wept some days to watch
his long waiting, sonorous mumbling
prayer trailing into sleep. For many
months he has wished to be
dismissed in peace.

Now, holding this child,
he can let go.

Glad for his good release, I mourn
the mother's pain, the child's plight,
the loss that comes
for me in this: no longer to see him
on the Temple steps, old eyes glittering
with hope, always ready to retell
the ancient tales while doves coo
in the courtyard and chattering housewives
pass in the street and within
the drone of prayer turns story into song.

What darkness comes with this light
burden he bears now, gurgling
his brief contentment. Glory of Israel,
Revelation to the Gentiles, this little gift
of God will cost us all we know. I see
the sword in his mother's heart,
and in his own — and mine, too,
as the old man, his long watch ended,
speaks his fateful benediction.

Head
of
Christ

What he sees he takes in.
Every human sorrow
fuels the fire that burns
low and steady
in his open heart.

He looked at the leper like this,
imagining the man's life
before he changed it.

He looked at the centurion and saw
what it must be for a father
to watch his child die.

He looked at the woman by the well,
saw her five husbands, and sent her home
with a promise; at the woman caught
in adultery, and did not condemn her;
at the woman weeping at his feet — knowing
she knew him, who walked the dusty earth
unrecognized — and honored her extravagance.

One might live long
just to be looked at once this way,
judged, forgiven, and blessed,
taken in, recognized — a prayer answered
in eyes that meet longing and assuage it:
"Lord, remember me
when you come into your kingdom."

Jesus and the Woman at the Well

You never know who will be chosen.
A lot of folks who would have loved
to spend half an hour with God Incarnate
didn't get to.
        A lot of those
who had their moment with the Lord
never made it into history. Lost pearls,
those words exchanged along the dusty roads
that no one wrote down.

Then there's this woman. She's not a seeker.
She's just tired of coming all this way
for water, tired of men who take more
than they give, tired of righteous people
who still have their reputations.

She's no Rebekah, virginal and fair,
nor Rachel, ripe for love, ready with her water jar,
nor Zipporah, grateful for deliverance.

What mockery even to imagine her
among those holy women who found
their bridegrooms waiting by the well.

Baffled again, the disciples wondered:
*Why should she be an object of such attention —
not only Samaritan, but a woman,
and angry as a shrew? At least the whores
had a little laughter in them.*

Odd how he'll talk to anyone.
Could get him into real trouble
one of these days.
                    Not to mention
the embarrassment for the rest of us.

The Return of the Prodigal Son

We would expect a close-up:
"Father and son reconciled."
We would emphasize the intimacy
we've learned to invade:
the father's painful, joyful gaze,
the hands that draw his boy close
to the very heart he broke,
the young man's shame
in the shadow of a half-turned face.

The dark onlookers seem
almost a mistake: they mar
the tenderness of what would play
so much better on an empty stage.

How jarring to be reminded
how little that is human is private.
There are witnesses and judgments,
costs and consequences.

The painter insists on this awkward point:
the father's forgiveness is not the whole story.
The spotlight that illumines the two of them,
their embrace the very form of forgiveness,
doesn't quite obscure the ones who stand and watch,
not quite so willing to receive the wretched sinner home.

They have accounts to settle, doubts about
a change that seems a little too dramatic.
They are men of common sense.
Their judgments are just and cautious —
all things considered, quite properly skeptical.

The young man will wear his past, a hair shirt,
under festal garments. He will bear his brother's
reasonable resentment and endure recrimination
from those who make him a measure of their virtue,
shielded in his shame by his father's blessing,
girded with love for the hard labor to come.

Peter's Denial

Failing this test,
the rest of his life
he will remember:

he has no stones to throw —
not at liars or cowards,
the expedient, the self-serving,
hypocrites, dissemblers,
profiteers who trade on
the pearl of great price.

Having to live with
having denied the Lord,
in every evening's firelight
having to remember the heat
of this moment by the courtyard fire,

he will have to find his power
in penitence, his preaching fueled
by forgiveness, his message
amazing grace.

In his outstretched hand
he seems to hold the Lord himself
in the balance.
                    Even as he turns away
from the one whose love costs more
than he had reckoned, his body remembers
sinking in the waves: how the Lord took
the hand he stretched out then
and saved him from his unbelief.

Christk
on the
Cross
(1631)

Fully human, fully God.
The one claim is clear enough,
the other so at odds with this
tortured image of defeat, only faith
could possibly consent.

Painters go at it again and again,
the paradox of Spirit leaving flesh,
luminous and torn, all-knowing
and abandoned.

Jesus cries out. He hangs
in ominous twilight.
The only light left
in an angry heaven
turns his flesh to gold.

What must the prayer of the painter be
who takes on such a task?

Let my hand not recoil
from the body's truth,
nor my brush stray
from the story.
Let me be true to the darkness
you entered, O light of the world,
and to the awful beauty
of your agony.

Christic at Emmaus

Christ

at

Emmaus

(1628)

One of them recoils.
One buries his head in the Lord's broad lap.

What would you do
if, mid-meal, light suddenly broke
from a body rather like your own

and a stranger suddenly became
in very flesh the friend you mourned?

You would be shocked, no doubt — horror,
amazement, joy, dismay competing,
no words available for the occasion.

You might embrace him, weeping,
or grasp instead at some shred
of rationality while your pupils
contracted and your heart beat in your throat.

It might be harder than you think
to give up three days' mourning,
memories already being edited and arranged.

The story had seemed complete.
Having a tale to tell, you might already
have found a way to tell it whole,
rich with mystery, rounded and
resonant with meaning.

You might have been ready
to go back home, tired of all that wandering,
ready to sit at the lakeside and take up
the nets again, writing a little, keeping
your counsel, sharing a parable now and then
with those who had seen him once,
who remembered the picnic on the hillside —
all that bread and fish.

You would have had to give up yet again
what you thought you had a right to claim.
Turns out he meant it — the promise
you'd already begun to turn to metaphor.

Here in dazzling flesh, leaning back
to let himself be seen, he leaves them no choice
but to lay aside sweet sorrow and cancel all their plans
for the aftermath.

Peter and Paul Disputing

(The Hebrew subtitles in this poem represent the four levels of interpretation recognized in traditional Jewish scholarship. Together they make an acronym, roughly transliterated as PRDS, standing for "paradise.")

P'SHAT, פְּשָׁט *(the literal)*
Plain sense? He never made plain
sense. Words that seemed simple
turned strange. When he spoke
my name, I felt God's thumb
making me out of mud. A blessing
over a couple of dried fish
almost caused a riot. Now I take
even bald facts on faith. I know
nothing I knew before,
and much more.
                    Don't quibble.
A sentence is five loaves.

REMEZ, רֶמֶז *(hints)*
I'm not quibbling.
After what I've seen, every word
is precious. All that Torah,
and now this: a few ragged speeches,
bits of tales remembered
on the road, love lurking
in rebuke, not one word
only what it seems. You wrestle
with your memories; what I remember,
a voice that made a wilderness
of everything but love.

DRASH, דְּרַשׁ (story)
Start again, then. Imagine:
What could a fig tree be about?
How many ways can a man be born?
Are the jots and tittles stitches
on a king's robe?
Is every star a sign?

SOD, סוֹד (mystery, secret)
Sometimes I have to close the book.
Its silence deafens me; it drives me mad.
Someone absconded, left a few crumbs
in the path — not enough to satisfy
anyone but a fool. And yet, to read it
is paradise already.

Self-Portrait as the Apostle Paul

Not how I imagine Paul,
yet these are eyes that might have seen
all the follies of Corinth, and found them
pitiable — trying, mostly —
and really, after all, a bore.
This face, the face of one who has learned
patience — had to learn it — listening
to local wrangles, refereeing factions
among the faithful, Jews
and Greeks, meat-eaters and righteous
abstainers who go green at the thought
of a slaughtered pig.

The thorn in his flesh throbs
in the long nights, on the road
from Ephesus to Philippi.
His lamp burns late, evenings,
as he bends over letters
to confused congregations who await
his word, barely beginning
to understand, not at all sure
they even want to know
what he has to tell them.
His daily discipline to feed
the sheep, trying not to think
of them as swine among the pearls.

No sentimentalist, he knows love
is patient, kind, and beareth all things
but does not need to suffer fools
or give up a good argument
for the sake of spurious peace.

63

The light that blinded him,
bearable now where he sits
in the shadows pondering,
falls on the open page,
and all his words, like Thomas's,
suddenly seem like straw.

Self- Portrait

(1669)

One last look in the mirror
the year of his death
shows not just
what time and tragedy have done,
but what survives the darkness,
and still defies the gravity
that pulls the aging body
toward the grave.

Cocky hat, coiffed hair,
neat tucked collar frame a face
full of years and sorrow, but still
searching, alert to what may meet
the curious and willing eye.

His gaze is disconcerting — a confrontation,
an invitation: look. If you have eyes
to see, be watchful. Peer
into the shadows. Bless the body
in its age, in its pain, for bearing
the light awhile, flesh like the grass
turning once more to the sun before
the wind blows, and it is gone.

LIST OF ILLUSTRATIONS

Page 13: Detail of *Two Scholars Disputing,* c. 1628, National Gallery of Victoria, Melbourne, Australia/Bridgeman Art Library.

Page 14: *Self-Portrait,* c. 1628, Staatliche Kunstsammlungen, Kassel, Germany.

Page 16: *Woman Bathing in a Stream,* c. 1654, National Gallery, London, UK/Bridgeman Art Library.

Page 18: *Sacrifice of Isaac,* c. 1635, Scala/Art Resource, NY.

Page 21: Detail of *Sacrifice of Isaac.*

Page 22: *Jacob Wrestling with the Angel,* c. 1660, Staatliche Museen, Berlin, Germany/Bridgeman Art Library.

Page 24: *Jacob Blessing the Children of Joseph,* c. 1656, Gemaldegalerie, Kassel, Germany/Bridgeman Art Library.

Page 27: Detail of *Jacob Blessing the Children of Joseph.*

Page 28: *Moses Smashing the Tablets of the Law,* c. 1659, Gemaldegalerie, Berlin, Germany/Bridgeman Art Library.

Page 31: Detail of *Moses Smashing the Tablets of the Law.*

Page 32: *Hannah and Samuel,* c. 1648, Duke of Sutherland Collection, on loan to the National Gallery of Scotland.

Page 34: *The Reconciliation of David and Absalom,* c. 1642, Hermitage, St. Petersburg, Russia/Bridgeman Art Library.

Page 36: *Simeon with the Christ Child,* c. 1669, Nationalmuseum, Stockholm, Sweden/Bridgeman Art Library.

Page 38: Detail of *Simeon with the Christ Child.*

Page 40: *Head of Christ,* c. 1650, Gemaldegalerie, Berlin, Germany/Bridgeman Art Library.

Page 42: *Christ and the Woman of Samaria,* c. 1655, Staatliche Museen, Berlin, Germany.

Page 45: Detail of *Christ and the Woman of Samaria.*

Page 46: *The Return of the Prodigal Son,* c. 1668, Scala/Art Resource, NY.

Page 49: Detail of *The Return of the Prodigal Son.*

Page 50: *The Apostle Peter Denying Christ,* c. 1660, Rijksmuseum, Amsterdam, Holland/Bridgeman Art Library.

Page 52: *Christ on the Cross,* c. 1631, Eglise du Mas d'Agenais, France/Giraudon-Bridgeman Art Library.

Pages 54-55: *Christ at Emmaus,* c. 1628, Musee Jacquemart-Andre, Paris, France/Art Resource, NY.

Page 58: *Two Scholars Disputing,* c. 1628, National Gallery of Victoria, Melbourne, Australia/Bridgeman Art Library.

Page 61: Detail of *Two Scholars Disputing.*

Page 62: *Self-Portrait as the Apostle Paul,* c. 1661, Rijksmuseum, Amsterdam, Holland.

Page 65: Detail of *Self-Portrait as the Apostle Paul.*

Page 66: *Self-Portrait,* c. 1669, Scala/Art Resource, NY.

W9-BZB-907